Grandpa Jack's Bitcoin Dialogues

Bitcoin's Value for Boomers and Others

Ben Theyre

Dedication

To Marianna, my wife and ever-skeptic of Bitcoin, this book is dedicated to you.

To my children, their spouses, my grandchildren, and my close friends—your encouragement has been invaluable in the writing of this book. Thank you.

Table of Contents

Introduction

Meet Fred and Jack, two friends who are retired and enjoy having breakfast together each week. Their conversations take place in a café and during walks after breakfast. They talk about the various goings-on in their lives, but one of the characters is a Bitcoiner—he buys and holds bitcoins. After this is revealed, the other friend experiences shock and later curiosity. Each week they talk about many things, but different aspects of Bitcoin are weaved into their weekly dialogue. Their conversations are not about technology; they are about the practical reasons for owning some bitcoin, even at their age, according to one of the characters.

Chapter 1:

Two Old Men Who Meet

for Breakfast

T he fog was thick—only here in the Pacific Northwest, we didn't call it fog. It was a *marine layer*. Today, it blanketed the shoreline, obscuring visibility across Saratoga Passage.

On a clear day, one could see from Mukilteo across the water to Clinton. These two towns hosted ferry terminals that received boats transporting people and vehicles between the mainland and Whidbey Island.

Jack sat in his truck listening to the pre-game show on the radio. The Mariners were on the road on the East Coast today. He was parked, waiting for the boat. Visibility was only about one hundred yards. The parking lot, terminal building, and pier were visible, but nothing farther away was. An ex-jock and a witty personality bantered back and forth on the radio about what the Seattle Mariners needed to do to get the team into the playoffs. In a black BMW parked next to him, a young woman talked animatedly on her phone. An elderly couple strolled by on the walkway in front of him. Off to his left, a man with two little girls in tow hurriedly walked toward the elevator leading up to the terminal entrance. *One of them needs to use the potty*, Jack thought with a smile as the scene brought back fond memories of his daughters at that age.

Suddenly, the ferry boat appeared in front of him. As in a movie or a dream-like state, one moment there was only fog; in the next moment, a large boat maneuvered to dock. Even though these boats were equipped with advanced radar navigation systems, Jack still admired the piloting skills of their human captains. He watched as the passenger bridge lowered onto the boat, enabling the walk-on passengers to disembark above the automobiles. When he saw his friend emerge, he started the truck and drove to the curb.

So began a weekly ritual. Two old friends of senior citizen age met on Wednesdays to have breakfast together. The weekly meetup had been going on for several years, but the routine changed slightly when Fred and Margo moved to Whidbey Island. Now, instead of meeting at a restaurant somewhere on the east side of Seattle, Fred walked on the ferry boat in Clinton, and Jack drove to Mukilteo to pick him up.

Fred waved as he descended the stairs of the terminal building and climbed into the truck.

"Good morning, Jackski," Fred said, wearing his usual smile.

"Top of the morning, Fredski," Jack answered. The two had appended "ski" to each other's names as a friendly greeting for an unremembered reason several years ago, and it had stuck.

They drove to Patty's Café. There, they cooked eggs the way Jack liked them: sunny side up with firm whites and soft yokes. At other restaurants, he would often get drippy whites or hard yokes when he ordered them that way.

Pulling open the glass door and entering the café, patrons' first impression was that the front section seemed narrow. The wall on the left side featured a row of windows with sun blinds pulled up, allowing in natural light. Tables and chairs next to the wall left a narrow walking path. On the right side, the cashier station was located about ten feet from the door. An open space between the cash register and the beginning of a counter where diners could choose to sit allowed wait staff to enter and exit the kitchen area. Farther down the walkway and past the end of the counter was a half-wall, open at the top, framing an entryway to a larger dining area. Before setting foot on the step down into this back dining room, a right turn would take you to a passageway between the wall and the end of the counter that led to the restrooms.

Jack and Fred didn't wait for host seating. They knew where they liked to sit. The two walked toward the back, stepped down, and entered the larger dining area. They picked a window table on the left side wall midway.

Leena, their favorite server, was working today. She always kept their coffee cups full. She stood about five feet tall. Soft green eyes peeked out from below bangs of auburn hair tied in a ponytail. An ever-present smile beamed from her oval-shaped face, projecting warmth and friendliness. Jack wished her voice more closely reflected her demeanor. Leena's natural voice was a few decibels higher than he preferred, *but we are all unique creatures*, he told himself.

Leena's smile grew wider when she recognized two of her favorite regular customers. She greeted them and brought them coffee. The coffee was always hot, fresh, and plentiful here. Jack liked coffee before he ate breakfast, while he was eating breakfast, and after he finished eating breakfast. Jack liked coffee.

He was not a fan of those fancy coffee specialty cafés, though. Coffee prepared with steamed milk and added flavors and sold with exotic names didn't impress him. He was of the mind that if coffee was ground from good beans and served fresh and hot, then it didn't need anything added to it. His wife, Mary, liked those coffee specialty drinks, though. Whenever he accompanied her to one of those places, he noticed that customers ordering drinks seemed to speak a unique language describing what they wanted. Mary was fluent in that lingo.

Eating out was always a risk and a compromise. You never knew if the food would be cooked to your liking or if the coffee would be a standard institutional blend or an upgrade, but if you were there with good company, then the risk and compromise were worth it. The two friends found Patty's food consistently good, and Jack rated the coffee "drinkable—above institutional blend."

After settling in and drinking some coffee, Fred asked, "Do you know my friend Carl?"

"I don't know him, but I've heard you mention him before," Jack responded.

"He and I went to the game last week," Fred announced. "Watched Kirby pitch a great game." He figured that would elicit an excited response from his friend.

Jack liked baseball and football but favored baseball. A lifelong fan of the game, he'd hoped to be a professional player when he was young, but he had discovered the world was filled with talent, so he'd had to figure out another way to earn a living. Today, he preferred to watch games on TV rather than go to the ballpark. He didn't like crowds and felt big league baseball was ripping off the fans with exorbitantly unreasonable prices for parking, admission, and concessions.

"I watched Kirby pitch a complete game a few weeks ago against Philadelphia. He fanned seven batters," Jack replied with predictable enthusiasm. "Between ticket prices and parking, I bet that set you back several hundred bucks."

"No, I got off cheaply. Someone gave Carl the tickets, and we took the light rail from North Seattle to the ballpark," Fred replied with a grin.

Leena appeared next to their table. "Have you two gents decided what you will have for breakfast?" she asked.

Jack ordered his customary two eggs sunny side up with the whites firm, bacon, hash brown potatoes, and rye toast. Breakfast was Jack's favorite meal of the day. Occasionally, he would have pancakes, but he didn't feel the need to experiment with different entrees since he knew what he liked. Fred ordered the daily special, a California omelet.

"It's funny—they add a slice of avocado and call it a California something or other," Jack mused. "I was born and raised there, but I don't remember eating many avocados."

"That's probably because you were born before they discovered avocados," Fred quipped.

Four elderly gentlemen sat at a nearby table. Fred and Jack had seen them on other visits to the café. One seemed to be a retired professor or teacher. He would talk about a book he read; another one seemed to talk about geopolitics; another was thought to be a musician, and the other one seemed to talk about spiritual things. Fred had come up with the musician label for the one guy because he overheard him talking to his companions about a gig he had played recently.

Each week, Jack and Fred talked about baseball, football, politics, family, personal events, the stock market, friends, new technology gadgets, and world events. Over the years, as they grew to know each other and felt comfortable with their friendship, they respected and tolerated each other's different opinions, and their conversations grew less superficial and more meaningful.

"Margo is getting so much out of her weekly therapy sessions. It is so great to see her come out of her shell and be comfortable with her gift," Fred told Jack after taking a sip of his coffee.

Fred's wife Margo was prescient but reluctant to speak up. As a child, she was often mocked when she predicted something. When, more likely than not, her premonitions came true, she was shunned by her friends who didn't know what to make of her remarkable gift. Later in life, she was moody and upset with herself because of her reticence in telling others of something she had seen, but the emotional pains suffered in childhood by her friends' reactions to her had left deep scars. She had confined the telling of her psychic visions only to her husband. These visions happened less frequently in Margo's life now. Sometimes years would separate them.

"She had another vision and told her friend Annie about it," Fred explained.

A light rain was falling outdoors, and water droplets streaked across the café windows. Jack sipped his coffee and listened as Fred described the changes in Margo as she emerged from her psychological shell.

"More coffee?" Leena asked, standing next to their table with a coffee pot in hand. Jack gladly accepted. Fred asked for decaf.

"Does she have any predictions for the stock market?" Jack asked, only partly tongue in cheek.

"No. I asked her that years ago when she first told me about her psychic abilities, but she said they are usually about people and sometimes events," Fred answered.

A family with young children entered and sat at a table nearby. A look of horror crossed both men's faces. "Why aren't they in school?" Fred whispered.

The children dressed as if they were going to a party. Each was wearing a colorful costume, and each had a different face mask. The youngest was unhappy about something and let everyone in the café know it. After what seemed like an eternity, which was only about thirty seconds of actual screaming, the mother picked up the child and took her outside. Jack was amused that the father had tried to reason with her while her wailing paused only long enough to inhale another lung full of oxygen. The little human air raid siren could be heard outside, but not loud enough to spoil everyone's breakfast. Diners resumed their chatter, and the noise level in the café returned to a normal din.

Leena brought their breakfast orders. Jack had been swimming before he drove to Mukilteo to pick up Fred. He was hungry and plunged his fork right into the eggs and potatoes on his plate.

Reaching for the salt and pepper, Fred asked, "How is your Microsoft stock doing?"

Jack bit into a piece of crispy bacon to buy some time before answering. Usually, they didn't talk about personal financial information unless it blended into a different topic they were discussing. Also, he had just made a change in his investments that he knew would provoke a reaction from his friend, so it was with reluctance that he answered.

"Actually, I sold it," Jack replied, hoping that would be the end of it.

"Knowing you, you bought something else. What did you buy?" Fred prodded while lifting his cup for another sip of coffee.

Jack lifted his cup, took a sip, and said, "Bitcoin."

Fred coughed as he attempted to swallow his coffee. His eyes widened. After a few seconds, he put down his cup, wiped his mouth with his napkin, looked at his friend, and cast about for something to say. "Doesn't that price volatility scare the hell out of you? I heard the price can move a few thousand dollars in a day," Fred responded after recovering from his gasp.

"Yes, it can do that," Jack said. "Before I really understood Bitcoin, the price movement used to bother me. But I get it now, so I look at price declines as bitcoin being on sale and I buy more. Besides, if you were charting its price history, you would see it has trended up and to the right since its existence."

Fred stared in disbelief at his friend. He knew Jack was smart and did his research, but this left him completely unprepared. He didn't know what to say. Finally, he could only muster, "Well, I'm sure you did your homework on bitcoin. You wouldn't give up a solid stock like Microsoft for it otherwise. Please tell me you investigated it in-depth before buying it," Fred pleaded.

"Hundreds, maybe even a thousand hours," Jack said reassuringly.

There was a long silence. Jack could tell this was a lot for his friend to process. He decided to change the subject. "Are you ready for a walk?" he asked. The companions usually went for a long walk after breakfast.

As regular customers of Patty's, they retrieved the café's punch cards from their wallets and presented them to the cashier with their credit cards. Fred bragged that he had only one more breakfast to get his card fully punched. That meant his next breakfast would be $5 off. Previously, they had joked about becoming stereotypical old guys looking for discounts. Jack recalled when he was younger and would stop someplace for breakfast, there was usually a table with some old guys wearing World War II hats and ordering off the senior menu. *It is our generation now,* Jack pointed out, that is the older cohort ordering off the senior menu. *Some of us wear Vietnam Vet hats.* Neither Fred nor Jack wore veteran hats, but sometimes they split a breakfast order, which was like getting a discount. Not that they hadn't served in the military—they both had—it was just that they didn't need any more reminders about getting older.

The rain let up, and the sun briefly appeared between the clouds as they set off on their post-breakfast walk.

"Looks like you won't need your Indiana Jones hat," Jack jibed at Fred. Gravel on the footpath made a crunching sound as they embarked on the trail. Fred carried an over-the-shoulder tan-colored leather bag with him. The bag's contents seem to vary from week to week, but a rain hat was a staple item. Jack liked to tease Fred about his topper but begrudgingly admired it. He wore a baseball cap.

"No, not today," Fred replied. They walked on awhile in silence.

"Well, I'm happy for Margo," Jack said, trying to make conversation.

"Thanks," Fred muttered.

After walking for a while on the path and ducking low-hanging tree branches, Fred asked, "What made you decide to put your money in Bitcoin?"

Jack thought for a while before answering. He was a details guy. He often thought like an engineer. He was one to read the fine print, and he liked to know how something worked. In the case of Bitcoin, he had studied it thoroughly. He'd read books and articles, and he'd watched hours of YouTube videos. He still did so he could keep up to date. After watching enough videos, he determined which presenters had credibility and which ones didn't. He narrowed his regular video-watching diet to about a dozen or so knowledgeable people. He learned how bitcoin scarcity increased every four years, how it was safe from hacking, how it was better than gold in protecting its owners from inflation, how the price volatility could work for you, and how it could not be confiscated by the government or anyone else. His friend, Fred, on the other hand, was not a details guy. He was more of a give-me-the-thirty thousand-foot-view type of thinker. One was not better than the other; it was just who a person was, that was all. Jack was glad their friendship allowed them these differences.

"Grandchildren and melting ice cubes," Jack replied.

Chapter 2:

Reciprocity

A confessed breakfast slut, Jack preferred breakfast meetings to lunch or dinner meetings. Former business colleagues knew they could entice him to attend a meeting if it was scheduled at breakfast time. After their business careers ended, Jack and Fred started meeting for coffee weekly. The coffee meetings graduated into breakfast meetings. They lost track of how many years they had maintained this tradition.

One afternoon, Jack's phone dinged, alerting him of a text message. Jack looked at the picture in the message: a couple of fried eggs atop mashed potatoes covered in country gravy, sliced sausage, rye toast, all garnished with a sprig of green. He smiled; his friend Fred knew how to get his attention.

When Fred's text message described this delicious breakfast he had at a new café in Langley, Jack knew it was his way of suggesting it was Jack's turn to go over to the island for breakfast.

Wednesday morning found Jack in the ferry building terminal attempting to purchase a ticket for the crossing to Clinton. On previous trips to the island, he'd bought the ticket from the kiosk machine and clicked on the senior citizen price, which cut the fare in half. That option was not displayed this morning. On a second attempt, Jack studied each screen on the machine carefully making sure he didn't miss it, but no such option presented itself. He was about to pay the full price when he noticed someone in the information booth. Before committing to the purchase, he walked over to the booth and inquired about the missing option on the ticket machine. The man behind the counter smiled broadly and informed Jack that they had removed it.

"Why?" Jack asked.

After a chuckle, the man replied, "We discovered that all of our walk-on passengers were senior citizens."

The man presented the reduced fare senior ticket. Jack thanked him and walked to the boarding line. Although happy to get the discount, he also felt another rude reminder of his having reached senior citizen status when the ticket agent didn't ask him for proof of his age. Aging happened in a stealth way. Also, it happened rapidly, like wild blackberry bushes that produce ripe and delicious fruit in August that is gone in September. *I still don't feel my age,* Jack thought. Then he heard a voice from within reminding him that that was something to be grateful for. "I am grateful," he whispered.

Walk-on passengers boarding a Washington state ferry boat from Mukilteo enjoyed a pleasant experience. The terminal was one of the newest in the ferry system and featured a covered passageway to the boarding ramp. Sitting in a small control booth at the end of the walkway, an attendant worked a panel of buttons and levers to lower an electro-mechanically controlled ramp onto the upper deck of the ferry boat. A crew member on the boat secured the ramp. After the last of the disembarking passengers exited, the embarking passengers took their turn to walk down the ramp to the boat. Simultaneously, automobiles were loading on the lower decks.

In years past, the upper deck had offered a canteen staffed with people serving hot beverages and a variety of sandwiches and snacks. However, since the pandemic had ended, the snack area was all vending machines. This was unimportant to Jack, since the crossing took less than fifteen minutes and he was going to meet Fred for breakfast. Only a few passengers milled about the lounge area this morning. There were many seats to choose from, and walking outside to stand on the deck was also an option. The weather today was cool, so Jack chose a window seat on the boat's starboard side. He pulled out his smartphone and sent Fred a message saying that he was onboard and the boat was underway.

Jack leaned back into the padded bench seat and looked through a large window, observing seagulls flying parallel to the boat. Their wings extended, they were gliding on a current of air, eyeing the water below them for a meal. While the birds were fully absorbed in the immediate task of finding food, they didn't know how magnificent they looked, Jack speculated.

The southern tip of Whidbey Island was rural, tree-lined, and sparsely populated. Most of the small family farms hiding behind tall trees were not visible to the traveler who only drove on the main north-south highway. As charming as this rustic setting was, Jack was displeased that most of the cafes didn't open until 11 a.m. In past trips, they might have driven thirty miles up the island to find an open café. This new one in Langley was an exception.

The boat docked at the Clinton terminal. Jack zipped his jacket and walked down to the car deck. There was no separate passenger loading/off-loading ramp at this old facility. Walk-on passengers gathered at the front of the boat, and the crew, after securing the mooring lines, motioned to them to leave ahead of the automobiles.

Jack circled the old terminal building and hiked up a hill to a parking area designated for passenger pick-up. He spotted Neville, the name Fred had given his 1996 dark green Silverado pick-up truck, parked by the curb.

"Good morning, Jackski," Fred said greeting his friend with a smile as Jack climbed into the truck.

"Top of the morning, Fredski," Jack replied.

"You're going to like this place," Fred said to set his friend's predisposition. "The food's good—biscuits melt in your mouth, and the coffee is hot." After years in the sales profession, Fred had learned to set the stage and create a favorable image in his customers' imaginations before presenting the product. "The only negative I've found so far—and I've only been there once—is the waitress isn't as good-looking as Leena." He laughed.

The café was small. It had six tables in the dining area. A counter area the length of the entry wall featured bakery goods. Sally introduced herself as their server by saying, "I'll be taking care of ya today." Jack wondered why the wait staff used that expression. It seemed universal. It seemed to him as though every waiter in the world was trained by the same person. He didn't need to be taken care of; all he wanted was a good breakfast and hot coffee. He worked to suppress his irritability. It wasn't Sally's fault that he didn't have a cup before leaving the house, or that he was by nature irritable on an empty stomach. Luckily, she brought their coffee quickly. Jack took his first sip and smiled. To him, few things in life compared with that first taste of exceptionally good-tasting coffee in the morning. He knew it would be good before even tasting it, as the aroma from the cup that greeted his sense of smell was magnified by the sensation of his taste buds when he swallowed the first sip.

"Hey, this is pretty darn good coffee," he blurted out. "It's not institutional blend like they serve in a lot of places."

Pleased to hear the compliment, Sally smiled and said, "No, we get it from a local roaster here on the island."

Fred grinned from across the table. "I knew you'd like it," he said, pleased with himself for recommending the place.

"Did you watch the game last night?" Jack asked.

"You bet! That was one game I was not going to miss," Fred replied.

Football season was underway, and the Seahawks had played Denver in the first Monday night game. This contest was widely anticipated in the Seattle area because their former legendary quarterback, Russell Wilson, had left the team and signed with the Denver Broncos. People who attended the game went there as much to boo Wilson as to root for the Seahawks. Fans watching TV were doing the same thing in their living rooms.

The experience reminded Jack of a similar event in baseball years before when Mariners' superstar, Alex Rodriquez, who was affectionately called "A-Rod," left the team when his contract expired and signed with the Texas Rangers for more than one-quarter of a billion dollars. Jack fondly remembered the next season when the Rangers came to Seattle to play the Mariners. He'd attended that game. When Alex took his first turn at bat, the booing was so loud it seemed to rattle Rodriquez. Fans were throwing Monopoly money at him and calling him unaffectionately "Pay-Rod."

"It turned out like a Hollywood script, didn't it?" Fred asked.

"Sports fans are like a woman scorned," Jack replied, referring to fan reaction to Wilson.

"Russ learned that last night, I bet," Fred replied with a grin.

The guys ate their breakfast while reconstructing Monday night's football game. After finishing his meal, Jack pushed his plate to the side and reached for his coffee cup. Fred pulled a ziploc plastic bag from his carry bag and poured out more than a dozen vitamin pills onto a napkin. At Patty's Café across the water, Leena would always bring a pitcher of water so Fred could refill his glass after he finished eating. Jack gave Fred his glass since he did not like to drink water.

"I know a great place to hike, and it is not far from here," Fred announced as they climbed into Neville. The old truck smoothly managed the winding narrow country roads and finally came to a stop in a dirt parking lot in front of the entrance to Putney Woods.

"It seems like there are a dozen trails that branch off from the main entrance," Fred said. "I think I've been on all of them. We'll take one today that doesn't have a steep ascent."

"That sounds good to me," Jack replied, still feeling full of breakfast.

Shortly after beginning their hike, Fred turned to Jack and said, "I'm still struggling with this whole Bitcoin thing. I mean, I get it up to a point. There is only a fixed number of coins that will be mined. As more people become aware of it, demand will grow, and the price will increase. But, jeez, how long will that take?"

Jack stepped over a fallen branch. "Keep in mind that Bitcoin is not just an American technology. It's available to all eight billion people on the planet," Jack replied. "Currently, nineteen million of the twenty-one million coins that will ever be mined are already in existence. Also, it has now caught the eye of financial institutions who are moving substantial amounts of capital to buy bitcoins. There are even ETF funds selling spot bitcoin exchange-traded funds."

Jack was pleased that Fred had been thinking about Bitcoin, but he didn't want to overload him with information. Although he liked talking about Bitcoin, Jack knew he could sometimes talk too much and overwhelm the listener. He thought it was best to just answer his friend's questions.

They hiked to a fork in the trail, where they paused to catch their breath. The path to the left was a long but safe and level switchback that gently looped around Western Red Cedar and Douglas Fir trees back to where they entered. The path to the right was a shorter distance to their objective, but it was not level; it was continuous ups and downs that could challenge the joints and muscles. Jack had been working out and felt he was in shape for either one but told Fred to pick the direction. Fred took it as a challenge. The guys might have been past their prime age, but not above a challenge.

Fred nodded his head toward the more arduous trail.

"Last week when I asked you why bitcoin, you said something about grandchildren and melting ice cubes. What did you mean?" Fred asked Jack as the two started down the rugged path.

After they topped the first hill, Jack responded, "Mary and I want to leave something specifically for the grandchildren. I think bitcoins are perfect for long-term holding. I expect them to appreciate over time, and time is something the grandchildren have in abundance."

The trail descending the downside of the hill was a steep angle. A narrow valley at the bottom would afford them only a brief respite before scaling up the next hill. Fred led the way, facing sideways, sliding his feet at an angle to slow his descent. They met at the bottom and paused before climbing the next hill.

"You could just put some money in a savings account or buy a bond for them," Fred said.

"Well, that's the melting ice cube part," Jack retorted.

Fred turned to Jack with a quizzical look on his face.

"Have you been in a grocery store lately?" Jack asked in his best non-offensive tone of voice. "Did you pay the same amount of money for your favorite loaf of bread recently that you paid last year, or the year before that?" After climbing up hills and skidding down hills, the two were sweating and in need of a breather but pressed on up the last hill. At the top, they stopped to catch their breath. The parking lot was in sight, and it was less than one hundred yards away on easy terrain to get there.

Always prepared, Fred had a couple of bottles of water in his haversack. He handed one to Jack and opened one for himself. They gulped down the water with gusto. *Phew!* It was an instant relief. Normally Jack didn't like drinking water, but he welcomed it now.

"So much for that easy ascent I promised you," Fred said laughingly.

After catching their breath and feeling refreshed, Jack decided to put the final point on his justification for buying bitcoins for the grandchildren.

"My view is that money is useful for daily transactions, but not for storing value over an extended period. Putting money in a savings account is like holding ice cubes in your hand. You can watch its purchasing power melt away. After all, what will that loaf of bread cost in ten or fifteen years?"

"I get your point," Fred acquiesced.

Jack realized his tendency to overtalk was emerging, so it was time to back off. "Hey, you want to race to your truck?" he asked teasingly.

Chapter 3:

Tractors

Leena's infectious laugh cackled from the other side of the café. She was flirting with a group of retired-age guys Jack and Fred had seen on previous visits to the café, barking out her unique laugh at their jokes. One of them was doing an impersonation of Jack Nicholson, a favorite of Leena's, and she responded with her own impersonation of the actor.

"I got the wheel spacers put on my tractor," Fred said proudly. "It feels more stable now when I'm mowing the embankment next to my house."

"Stability is a good thing," Jack responded after taking a drink of coffee from his cup.

"The tractor has a roll bar," Fred explained, "but I'd rather not have to test it."

Leena approached. "So, what are we having, boys?" she asked.

"How are the pancakes today?" Fred asked.

Turning her head slowly from one side to the other as if to make sure no one was listening, she bent over the table, cupped her hands around her mouth, and using a low whispered conspiratorial tone, said, "Truth is, they're about the same as they were yesterday." Her green eyes sparkled, and a smile widened her oval face.

Jack chuckled. He lowered his menu, turned his face to look up into Leena's eyes, and said, "Truth. You can't handle the truth!" He used his best Jack Nicholson impression.

Leena cackled loudly. "Oh, did you hear us talking about Jack Nicholson? Phil does a great imitation of him," she said.

Fred had a belly laugh at the whole scene, especially Leena's theatrics. He ordered the pancakes with eggs over easy, and Jack ordered his usual two eggs, sunny side up with firm whites, bacon, and rye toast. The jovial server memorized their orders, smiled, and said, "I'll be back." Leena's memory impressed the guys.

"Hey! That's not Nicholson, that's Schwarzenegger," Jack said loudly. Leena laughed as she walked away.

"So now we know one of those guys is called Phil," Fred said.

"Yeah, he is the quiet one, the guy doing the Nicholson impressions," Jack observed.

Setting down his coffee cup, Fred said, "Well, I have only one more thing to do to the tractor and then it will be ready for winter."

"What's that?" asked Jack.

"Put beet juice in the tires," he replied.

"Did you say beet juice?" Jack asked for clarification. "Why would you do that?"

"It gets back to that stability concept I like. It provides better traction when the ground is wet and cold," Fred explained. "You've seen that embankment by the side of my house—imagine driving the tractor over that after a good rain."

Jack frowned after visualizing such a task.

"I bought a front plow to remove snow in the winter and leaves in the fall. I tell you, I had some close calls with gravity on that slope last year," Fred said. He spent several minutes describing a couple of times when he had the shovel on the tractor and how that had changed the center of gravity. He felt lucky he hadn't tipped it over. "Margo loves to drive it, and I'm glad she wants to help with the mowing, but she won't take it up the embankment. Of course, I will still do the hillside even after I put beet juice in the tires."

Jack thought he was glad to be living in an urban area and didn't need a tractor to mow his lawn.

Leena's cheery voice announced the arrival of breakfast. "I'll be back with more coffee," she said after setting down their plates.

"I'll switch to decaf," Fred said.

After taking a few bites of his eggs and pancakes, Fred began talking about a book he was reading on Bitcoin. He hadn't finished the book yet but said he was at the part where the author was describing the hash wars.

"Ah, you must be around circa 2017 or '18," Jack piped up.

"Yeah, apparently there were a couple of hard forks in the network. One was called Bitcoin Cash, or BCH, and another was called Bitcoin Satoshi Vision, or BSV, if I remember correctly." Fred continued, "Save me some reading time—how did it end?"

"The short answer is the market, which is the majority of the miners who produce bitcoins—BTC—decided not to change. While some miners accepted one or the other of the proposed forks, most stayed with the original Bitcoin, BTC," Jack explained, enjoying his eggs and hash brown potatoes.

"So, are those forked versions still around today?" Fred asked between bites of pancakes.

"Yes."

"What's the difference, then, between the versions?" Fred asked.

Fred's question was sincere, but the answer could get technical. As far as communicating Bitcoin's value proposition here, those technicalities were a distraction. He didn't want to go down that rabbit hole. Jack decided to focus on the important distinctions in terms of the way most people could relate to: the value bitcoin, or BTC, represented.

"The main differences are technical," Jack explained. "Mostly it is about the size of the blocks added to the block chain. It's the type of stuff techno-geeks argue about. For my money, BTC is valuable. The market has endorsed it, and that is good enough for me and my family's future. The bigger in size the Bitcoin network grows to, the safer it becomes. BCH has a market cap of about $10 billion, and BSV is around $50 or $60 billion, while BTC's market cap is currently greater than $1 trillion."

"Wow!" Fred sounded genuinely surprised that the market capitalization for Bitcoin was so large. "What do you think of those so-called altcoins? They are supposed to be alternatives to bitcoin."

"The way I look at it, there is no alternative to bitcoin," Jack said. "Some people trade altcoins, and I suppose some make money doing that, but I am not into trading. I prefer to HODL."

"HODL, what's that? Fred asked.

"Hold on for dear life," Jack replied. "For me, bitcoin is a savings account. I put any extra money I have into bitcoin." Jack lifted his cup for another gulp of coffee. "You could say bitcoin is like your tractor fully equipped with wheel spacers and beet juice in the tires," Jack added with a grin. "It has been through a lot and can take just about anything the world can dish out while providing safety and value."

Fred was quiet but looked intrigued. "Well, are you ready to take a walk?" he asked.

They hiked a familiar trail. It was mostly level and followed closely by the shoreline of Puget Sound. A high marine layer obscured the sun from view, but the air temperature was not cold. Jack wore a cotton sweater, and Fred donned a light jacket. The path paralleled close to the shoreline, and the smell of salt water was in the air. Jack commented that he felt at home being near salt water. They exchanged good morning greetings and smiles with others whom they passed by during their walk.

Chapter 4:

Another Wednesday Morning

Peple sitting at nearby tables looked up as the two senior citizens walked into Patty's and took a table in the back section of the café without being seated by a hostess. Fred and Jack laughed while speculating on the thoughts of their fellow diners.

"They probably think we own the place," Fred said with a chuckle.

As if to reinforce that image, Leena came to their table holding two mugs of coffee and set them on the table in front of Jack and Fred.

"Good morning, boys," Leena greeted them in a cheerful voice, wearing a big smile. The scene was a moment in time, and soon the other patrons were into separate conversations and enjoying their breakfasts.

"I remember going into coffee shops when I was younger and seeing old guys sitting around a table talking about all sorts of stuff, especially their aches and pains," Jack recalled.

"Me too," Fred agreed. "So, I won't talk about my sore thumb today." He grinned. The two men chuckled.

"Although it is keeping me from playing my guitar. But the good news is, I found a physical therapist who can help me with it. She is a musician herself."

"Another difference is we are not wearing veterans' hats," Jack observed. "When we were younger, some of those old guys had hats with the names of battleships they served on in World War II," he said. "Nowadays, our generation is the "older guys", and some men just wear a cap that says Vietnam Vet."

They sipped their coffee and studied the menu. "Hey, you want to split something?" Fred asked.

"Maybe. What do you have in mind?" Jack inquired.

"Take a look at that Mexican Omelet," Fred said pointing to an item on the menu. "It's got sausage, cheese, chili pepper, and avocado. It looks good, but is almost too much to eat by myself," Fred said half longingly and half pleading.

"Sure. Let's give it a try," Jack agreed. Leena came by the table and took their order.

Fred removed his black nylon piled jacket and hung it on the chair next to him at the table. He wore a light blue colored shirt imprinted with a mountain scene and the words *Life is Good* displayed below the mountain. Fred liked the shirt and had several of them. The message resonated with his belief.

Not a lot of diners today, so neighboring conversations can be easily heard. A group of four men sat at a nearby table.

"Did you guys read the passage I sent you?" inquired the presumed retired teacher of his breakfast companions who were busily eating their breakfasts.

These fellows had been here before at the same time as Jack and Fred, who often speculated on their backgrounds. Occasionally they heard a clue that might reveal something about them. They were reasonably certain that the one speaking, a distinguished-looking gentleman with white hair of medium length and neatly groomed, was a retired schoolteacher. Their private nickname for him was "the professor." They noted that he often cited books about whatever subject they were talking about. After noticing them several times during their weekly breakfast meetings, Jack and Fred were still comparing notes about them. One of the other guys had a full head of wavy black hair with only traces of silver, hinting that he might qualify for senior discounts, but his face projected that of a younger man. Fred and Jack speculated that this one was a musician. On one occasion, Fred heard him referencing a "gig" he had over a weekend, and one time he was trying out lyrics for a song he was composing. Still unresolved were two others. The tallest guy had white hair and a neatly trimmed white beard. He possessed a friendly countenance and looked like someone whom you would want to play Santa Claus at your Christmas party. The fourth guy in the group was quiet and sported a full head of black and silver hair with a matching beard. He seemed to listen more than talk.

"Here you go, fellas," Leena announced the arrival of their breakfast. "I'll be back with more coffee, is there anything else I can get you?"

Jack shook his head while Fred said, "I'd like to switch to decaf."

"Well, I did it!" Fred proclaimed with a wide smile after Leena had left.

Jack looked up from his eggs and asked, "You did what?"

"I bought some bitcoin," he said proudly.

"Congratulations," Jack was genuinely surprised. He thought of Fred as politically progressive but, when it came to his own money, financially conservative.

"What made you buy it?" Jack asked while reaching for his coffee cup.

"Well, I thought about the things we talked about—its scarcity, the large amount of institutional money buying it, and so on. Also, I watched some of the videos you suggested, but I started thinking about the inflation aspect. You know, I think inflation is higher than the government is telling us. If this keeps up, I could outlive my money," Fred explained.

"Did you buy a cold storage wallet? Jack asked.

"No, I just put a small amount of money into Bitcoin and will leave it on the exchange for now," Fred responded. "If something should happen to me, Margo can access the exchange account easier than she could a cold storage wallet."

Jack nodded in understanding.

"If I get comfortable with Bitcoin and decide to put more in, then I'll reconsider using a wallet. I can get my son to help me set it up," Fred explained. After swallowing a fork full of hash browns and a gulp of coffee, he continued, "I watched a video on a cold storage wallet setup. Margo is comfortable using the computer, but she might need help retrieving bitcoin from the wallet. It would give me peace of mind to have Pete there to help her."

One of the four guys, the "musician," broke into a song he had written. He had been telling his friends about a gig he performed last weekend, and he included a song of his own. The singing began. Another guy in their group, the big guy, said he liked to sing, too, and started singing the melody. All the diners laid down their forks and listened attentively. Applause broke out when the musician finished his song.

After listening to the *a cappella* singing, Leena arrived with more coffee. "Regular and decaf for you," she said looking at Fred as she brought him a fresh cup. She scampered away, joking with the four guys at the other table and complimenting them on their singing performance. They were getting ready to leave. They stood up, faced Leena, and in perfect harmony, sang a song from the movie, *The Sound of Music*.

"So long, farewell, *auf wiedersehen, adieu*," they sang as they walked away from their table. Continuing to walk toward the door, they made eye contact with other diners, including Fred and Jack, and pointed to them as they sang, "*Adieu, adieu*, to you and you and you." They left the café to a round of applause and appreciation.

Jack and Fred joined the applause and smiled at their performance. "Who are those guys?" Jack asked.

"I don't know, but we should get to know them the next time we see them here," Fred replied.

Jack nodded in agreement as he reached for his coffee cup.

While on their walk after breakfast, Fred was quieter than was his customary nature. Jack noticed a pensive look on his face. Other than some occasional small talk and acknowledging passersby, they didn't speak much until they got to a pier, where they walked toward its endpoint. Seagulls flew just above the water, scouting for food. Perched atop a piling supporting the pier was a plump seagull. He looked well-fed. The friends didn't want to frighten the bird, so they halted in place and gave it some space. The gull had been looking at them suspiciously as if deciding between staying put or flying away. When the guys stopped walking forward, the bird relaxed its feathers but kept an eye on them.

Not wanting to disturb the resting seagull, Jack and Fred turned back and retraced their steps on the pier. "You know, I'm glad I bought bitcoin for the reason I told you. Something that can protect savings from long-term inflation is reason enough for me. But Margo had another premonition. She didn't want to tell me all of what she saw but told me emphatically to buy bitcoin. She was so much in favor of it that I actually bought more than I originally intended to buy," he said, somewhat astonished by his action.

Now it was Jack's turn to be quiet. He maintained a macro view of business trends and world affairs. Sometimes this could be depressing. It was one of the reasons he looked forward to this weekly breakfast with Fred.

Chapter 5:

After the Visit Back East

L eena greeted Jack and Fred with a big smile and brought them coffee as soon as they found a table. Warm coffee mugs comforted their cold hands on this rainy morning. The café was busy. Most of the tables and booths were full of diners laughing and talking over breakfast plates. Outside rain splashed off the windows.

A grandfather clock standing in the corner seemed to be slowing down, Fred observed, looking at his watch and reaching for the warmth of his coffee cup.

"It's just like the rest of us; it's getting old," Jack responded.

Due to vacation trips, the men hadn't seen each other in nearly a month. "OK, I've been waiting to hear all about your trip. Do you still think ten days is too long to stay at someone's house as a guest?" Fred inquired of Jack.

He was referring to a previous conversation they'd had at one of their breakfast meetings when Fred was planning to visit friends and family in Oregon. He'd told Jack he would be staying for two weeks with his cousin. Staying at someone's house for more than two nights was inconceivable to Jack, let alone two weeks. He had communicated his opinion over coffee and pancakes that day. A few weeks later, when planning a trip back East to see one of his daughters, he'd had to reconsider his position when she implored him to stay for ten days.

"It depends on who it is, and it's not something I would do often,' Jack replied, "but I have to admit, it was a nice visit." He went on to describe some of the highlights of his trip to New England.

"So, what's for breakfast, boys?" Leena interrupted. She materialized seemingly out of nowhere from Jack's peripheral vision as he was recollecting memories of his trip. They placed their orders.

"More coffee?" Leena asked.

Jack nodded affirmatively. "I'll switch to decaf," Fred said.

"So, after all is said and done, the time did go by quickly," Jack continued. "We both like to walk, and we did a lot of walking on the beach. Also, we went to several places, but the time I value the most was the mornings we had coffee on her front porch and just talked. Here was this young woman talking about adult stuff, but whenever I looked at her, I just saw my little girl," Jack concluded.

There was silence for a few moments as they drank coffee.

"I know what you mean. My daughter is 36 and leads a hectic life, but she still reminds me of that child who just wanted to bring home every stray dog and cat in the neighborhood," Fred said.

"I'm going to have a similar experience again next week. I told you Rebecca, my oldest daughter, and her family have moved to Oregon. Her husband is climbing the executive ranks at his company, so they have moved around a lot the past few years. We were excited to learn they were moving back to the West Coast. They are finally settled in their new home, so Mary and I are going to drive down for a couple of days. I have a feeling the grandkids have grown considerably since we last saw them," Jack announced.

"Well, as a native Oregonian, I'm glad they settled there, too," Fred said. "So, I take it we are not meeting for breakfast next week?" Fred grinned.

"Not unless you want to come to Oregon," Jack replied with a smile.

"I do have family there, but I just got back from a long visit with them," he said.

At a nearby table, two guys whose ages appeared to be mid-twenties were talking about Bitcoin and cryptocurrency. One man wearing an orange-colored hoodie sweatshirt told his companion, "The difference between Bitcoin and all those shit coins is Bitcoin has no CEO, no management team, it is not a company, there is no one who can arbitrarily decide to mine more coins, and it is decentralized," he said in a very matter-of-fact tone of voice.

Jack turned his head to get a glance at the two men. He could see the Bitcoiner sitting erect in his chair, holding a piece of wheat toast in his left hand, a fork full of potatoes in the other hand, his head cocked to one side while he lectured his breakfast companion on the virtues of Bitcoin. His eyebrows arched up to nearly touch the tassels of his black curly hair. It was the look of the self-righteous who encountered a barbarian.

Jack only got a glimpse of the two breakfast companions when he turned quickly to sneak a peek at them. The other man was wearing a red squared flannel shirt with blond hair falling from his baseball cap and ending above the collar of his shirt. He was slumped over his plate. Defensively, the guy said, "Well, I think this one has a practical use case. It provides functionality that could help migrate tradfi—traditional finance—to crypto." He expressed himself sheepishly.

"Dude, first, I don't like to hear Bitcoin categorized with cryptocurrency. It is like taking something pure and clean and dragging it through a mud puddle. Secondly, while I don't know about the coin you're describing—there are only, what is the count now, 30,000 of those shit coins," he exclaimed. A shit coin was a derisive term used to describe cryptocurrency coins other than Bitcoin. Another term used in polite company was altcoin. "Most of those are pump and dump schemes," he proclaimed passionately.

"What do you mean?" asked the other fellow.

The Bitcoiner continued, "Look, making a shit coin is a relatively easy task for a good coder. So, after they create it, the initial investors receive a boatload of the coins, then they create a lot of marketing hype around it, the general public starts buying them, the price starts to move up, and then the initial investors dump their coins at a nice profit, leaving everyone else holding the bag," he explained.

Both men overheard the conversation. Jack smiled. He agreed with the Bitcoiner but thought a gentler approach would have been more effective in communicating Bitcoin's value to his friend. Still, he wasn't critical of the guy in the orange hoodie and was glad to see young people who were passionate about Bitcoin.

Leena brought their breakfast orders.

"What do you know about rats?" Fred asked.

"I know I don't particularly like them," Jack replied with a quick smile. "Why?"

"We have one in our attic. The little bugger is scratching on the floor above our bedroom. The noise is keeping Margo awake at night," Fred said. "I set traps, but he has eluded them so far."

"Pass the salt and pepper, please," Jack said.

Leena arrived with more coffee. "Here you go, boys." She scampered away, flirting with her male customers and complimenting her female patrons.

"They do have those electronic devices," Jack stated.

"Yeah, I put some on the outside of the house, but this rat found a different way in. I don't have an outlet in the attic so I need to wire one in before I can put one up there."

Leena brought menus to a young couple who took the booth behind Fred. Long brown hair parted in the middle of her head and falling to her shoulders, the woman leaned forward as she studied the menu through thin, black-framed glasses with round lenses. Her companion said something to her. She raised her head and responded with a delicate smile under a turned-up nose and sparkling blue eyes. Jack observed her while looking over Fred's shoulder. The guy she was with barely glanced at the menu before tossing it aside. He wore a white baseball cap.

"I'm gonna do it myself instead of hiring a contractor," Fred said.

"Huh?" Jack said distractedly.

"The wiring in the attic," Fred replied.

"Oh, I didn't know you were an electrician," Jack said, returning his attention from gazing at the attractive woman in the next booth.

"I'm not, but I think I can string the wire," Fred said.

The Bitcoiner and his cryptocurrency buddy finished their breakfasts and walked to the front to pay their check.

"I remember hearing that 'pump and dump' reference on some Bitcoin videos I watched," Fred said between bites of sausage and eggs.

"Sadly, 'pump and dump' has described many first-round investors in cryptocurrency projects. They get rich, and then others who come in afterward are left holding the bag when the price drops through the floor," Jack explained.

"That sounds like a Ponzi scheme," Fred observed. Jack nodded and wolfed down his remaining eggs and toast.

"Aren't Bitcoin and other cryptocurrencies regulated by the SEC?" Fred asked.

"Bitcoin is considered property by the SEC and the IRS. It's a commodity, not a security. However, the regulators take a different approach toward other cryptocurrencies," Jack explained. "The irony is that the industry, including the exchanges that sell these cryptocurrencies, want regulatory clarity. They have lobbied the SEC and Congress for it, to no avail. Instead of working with the industry to establish rules and regulations for consumer protection and other guidelines, the SEC has been hostile. They just sue cryptocurrency companies instead of providing guidance. It's regulation by litigation."

"That doesn't seem fair," Fred said indignantly. "What will it take to change that?"

"Probably a new administration, one that is crypto-friendly," Jack replied.

"Also, I thought it was interesting that the fellow took offense to his friend placing Bitcoin in the cryptocurrency category," Fred observed.

Jack swallowed a gulp of coffee and said, "Yeah, he is probably a Bitcoin maximalist. They see Bitcoin as the only cryptocurrency that will ever be needed in the future."

"Is that because it was the first one?" Fred asked.

"That's one reason," Jack answered. "There is a first-mover advantage. Bitcoin has the largest network and the largest market capitalization. Also, remember that it is decentralized and peer-to-peer. No company or individual controls it, which means no one can create more bitcoins. It is capped by the protocol at twenty-one million coins. There will never be any more than that."

Fred said the Bitcoiner sounded like a true believer.

In response, Jack said, "I don't want to carry the religious analogy too far, but there is that 'lightbulb' moment, that epiphany, that some people experience when they really understand Bitcoin."

Patty's quieted down as several patrons left. The men finished eating and got up to don their jackets and leave. As he slipped his arms into the sleeves of his coat, Jack looked down and made eye contact with the attractive-looking woman seated in the next booth. She smiled. He returned the smile and felt an extra bounce in his step as he walked toward the cash register. He thought the day was starting well.

After breakfast, they walked along the shoreline of Puget Sound and paused to take in the view. The morning's marine layer was gone, replaced by the sun, which warmed the air. A white ferry boat with green painted trim was approaching the dock. Farther along, the gravel and dirt pathway turned into smooth concrete, and soon they were standing in front of Mukilteo Terminal. Here, the two friends would say goodbye and part company until the next Wednesday morning. There might be an occasional text message or phone call in between.

Fred was taller than Jack and had a large frame. A full head of white hair made him stand out in a crowd, and when his beard wasn't trimmed, he looked like a mountain man. However, one look at his handsome face and sparkling blue eyes revealed a true gentle nature. One distinctive characteristic about Fred is that he was a hugger. When he said hello or goodbye to someone, it was always with a hug. It had taken Jack several years to adjust to this. It wasn't just because Fred was taller than him. No, it was just the whole two-guys-hugging thing. Both men had grown up in the 1950s and '60s era. Fred overcame that before Jack did.

Chapter 6:

Addiction, Exercise, and

New Thoughts on Money

I n the early part of the twenty-first century in America, it seemed every family had a relative, or knew someone, who suffered from drug or alcohol addiction. No socio-economic strata of American life were exempt.

"How is Robby doing?" Fred asked.

Jack shrugged. "We never hear from him unless he wants money."

"I hope you're not giving it to him," Fred retorted unhesitatingly.

Leena projected warmth at whomever she was speaking to. She came to their table with menus and to take their beverage orders. "I assume you boys want coffee," she said knowingly. Their favorite waitress possessed an infectious laugh and an enviable memory; she recalled customers' names and little tidbits of conversation she had with them regardless of how long ago it might have been since their last encounter.

Both men nodded in the affirmative. Leena left to fetch coffee and give them a few minutes to decide what they wanted to eat.

"No, his grandmother cut him off. She had a come-to-Jesus talk with him and told him she knew what he bought with money she had given him. She told him she had thought about it and how she did not want to be the one who gave him money he used to buy drugs that killed him," Jack shared.

Jack's grandson, Robby, had recently been released from the hospital. He had been found by someone lying in a coma-like state and unresponsive. In addition to his being addicted to illegal substances, he had other medical problems that increased mortality risks from drug abuse.

"The thing is, they will tell you what you want to hear. They will also steal you blind. I know people who have stolen from their mothers, fathers, siblings, spouses, best friends, to get money to buy drugs," Fred said.

"You know, this is not his first time in the hospital. He was there last year, too. The doctor told him then he would not live to his next birthday if he didn't stop using," Jack continued. "Sometimes I suspect he thinks he is invincible and wants to prove it."

"Well, he is not." Fred continued, "The numbers are only one in five he makes it."

Leena returned with their coffee and took their breakfast orders.

After sipping hot coffee from his cup, Jack asked "What do you mean by making it?"

"I mean getting clean… staying off drugs for at least five years. I'm twenty-six years sober and have mentored and sponsored many alcoholics over the years, and those are roughly the numbers that shake out," Fred said.

"But is alcoholism the same as drug addiction?" Jack asked.

"Buddy, I hate to tell you this, but the numbers are probably even more unfavorable for drug addiction," Fred said with conviction in his voice.

Jack sipped on his coffee and thought about it. Fred still attended AA meetings and was always available to help someone serious about turning their life around. He had previously shared how he had witnessed the tragedy of seeing guys apparently break free of the addiction, straighten out relationships with family and employers, and then make the mistake of thinking they could handle one drink in a social setting and find themselves falling off a cliff back into the grip of addiction. He said it takes almost superhuman effort to break free and climb back up that road to recovery. Fred told of someone he knew who went through the slip, slide, and climb back cycle more than a dozen times before finally staying sober.

Memories of Robby as a baby and small child flashed through Jack's mind. The boy had been happy and forthcoming. He would bounce around the aisles of a grocery store or in a public park and unabashedly share all the details about his life, tell you what he was thinking, and relate the most private information about his parents with anyone, including strangers, who made eye contact with him. A smile crossed Jack's face as some of the more humorous memories flooded his mind.

"Here you go. Sunny side up here and pancakes over here," Leena said as she correctly placed the dishes in front of the right person. "I'll be right back with more coffee," she said.

"I'd like to switch to decaf," Fred said.

"So, what determines who makes it and who doesn't? Is it pure chance?" Jack asked while reaching for his fork and knife.

"It is an individual thing," Fred tried to explain between bites of his pancakes. "A person must be determined to turn his life around. Also, there is something to be said for grace."

The men ate in silence for several minutes. Conversation could become heavy when it got personal. Jack knew of Fred's first-hand experience with alcoholism. Over the years, he had heard his friend describe his life as an alcoholic. He knew the regret he felt for the pain he'd caused in others.

He also knew all of the good Fred had done for others—being there for someone who had reached a point of despair and wanted with all their soul to turn it around but not knowing where or whom to turn to. Jack marveled at the patience it took to nurse someone along the road to recovery. He didn't know how Fred could go back time and again to support someone who made successful strides to beat the addiction only to then slide back down into the hell they were escaping from. Yet, Fred would be there for such a one. He had been there many times.

"You and Mary might want to go to an Al-Anon meeting," Fred said, breaking the silence. "You would find others who have experienced the same situation. It might help you with some ideas," he said encouragingly.

"I don't know why our society tolerates this. It's as though we stand around and watch all this crap come through our border and kill our children, but we do nothing about it," Jack protested.

"It's not the border; it's the big pharma companies," Fred retorted. "They manufacture opioids and then over-distribute them." Fred had passionate opinions about drug addiction and its causes. Currently, Fred's nephew was struggling to overcome an addiction to cocaine.

Jack saw they were looking at the problem from two different lenses. Both observations were true, but continuing with it would devolve into a political discussion. Normally he was fine with having that dialogue, but not today.

Leena came by to pour more coffee. They waved off the offer.

"Are you up for a walk today?" Jack asked.

"Of course. I look forward to it each week," Fred replied. He retrieved a folded round-shaped rain hat from his carrying bag and plopped it on his head. Jack donned his baseball cap.

After leaving the café, they decided to hike up a road that paralleled BNSF railroad tracks. The incline rate was steeper than it appeared at first glance, but the rain faded to a gentle mist, bringing cooling relief.

The occasional motorist driving up or down the road slowed to yield extra space to two old men acting like they were age thirty-something assaulting a hill with gusto, but who were made to realize they were no longer in their thirties.

After about a half-hour passed of slowly walking uphill, they were sweating and breathing hard. Fred suggested they take a break. On one side of the road, a cliff overlooked a westward view of Puget Sound. A low metal barrier afforded protection for people and vehicles that strayed too close to the cliff's edge. Looking west from this vantage point, the hikers caught their breaths and took in a generous view of Saratoga Passage. Pointing to the southern tip of Whidbey Island, Fred said, "There is Langley. You can't see my house, but that park is near it." Jack observed ferry boats circling wide apart from each other leaving from and coming to Mukilteo. Power boats and sailboats of different sizes cut across the paths of the ferry boats dotting the view. Occasionally, they would hear the distinctive warning sound of a fog horn when a boat would cross too close to the ferry.

"Do you ever miss California?" Fred asked.

Jack pointed to the view in front of them and said, "No. It's hard to beat this."

"Are you ready to turn around?" asked Fred.

Jack spied the Everett City Limit sign posted about twenty yards farther up the road. "Do you feel like walking up to that sign before turning around?" Jack inquired. "Then we can say we hiked through two cities today," he mused.

"Sure. Let's do it," Fred responded gamely.

Although small on the grand scale of worldly achievements, hiking up to the city limit sign before turning around felt exhilarating to these two senior citizens. During the descent on the paved road back to the parking lot, Fred told Jack about a guy he had been talking to on the boat coming over this morning. He told Fred that he trained himself to price everything in satoshis so he doesn't feel inflation.

"That's smart," Jack acknowledged.

"Remind me what a satoshi is again?" Fred inquired.

"It's the basic unit of a bitcoin. It is to a bitcoin what a penny is to a dollar," Jack replied. "Only instead of being one of one hundred, it is one of one hundred million."

"So, how does pricing something in satoshis insulate him from inflation?" Fred pursued.

"Bitcoin increases in value over time while the purchasing power of the dollar decreases," Jack explained. "So, it takes fewer bitcoins to buy something even if inflation has increased its dollar price."

Fred was bright and a quick study, but changing the way to think about money, after a lifetime of measuring everything in dollars and cents, required an adjustment to thought processes. The look on Fred's face suggested he was still working on adjusting that process. Jack felt his brief explanation of bitcoin pricing was not satisfactory. He suppressed his conscientious resolve to minimize overtalking a subject in favor of attempting a clearer explanation.

"Let me give you an example. Mary and I have a favorite brand of bread we buy at the store. Priced in bitcoin, last year that loaf would cost 11,000 satoshis, or sats. This year, the dollar price of that same loaf of bread increased twenty-one percent, but in bitcoin, the price dropped to 6,500 sats," Jack explained.

"Wow! I get it. That's a whole different way of looking at this inflation problem," Fred exclaimed.

"That's how Bitcoiners think about money. It is probably a good thing to practice, too," Jack added.

"That sounds ominous," Fred said.

"I don't mean it in a negative sense," Jack replied, "but if the maximalists are right, Bitcoin will eventually become a unit of account. We will start to see things priced in bitcoins. Already we are seeing merchants agreeing to take payment in bitcoins."

Exhausted from their hike, the sojourners arrived at the bottom of the steep road and walked to the parking lot. "Well, it wasn't like scaling Mount Everest, but I appreciated the exercise," Fred said as they piled into Jack's truck.

Jack drove Fred to the ferry terminal and said goodbye to his friend. He was listening to the radio on the drive home, but the news was all about war in Europe and soaring inflation in the United States. He switched off the radio.

www.ingramcontent.com/pod-product-compliance
Lightning Source LLC
Chambersburg PA
CBHW070354130626
46556CB00007B/3172